PORTRAIT OF
ST ALBANS

JUNE AND MICHAEL MASSEY

HALSGROVE

First published in Great Britain in 2010

British Library Cataloguing-in-Publication Data
A CIP record for this title is available from the British Library

ISBN 978 1 84114 909 7

HALSGROVE
Halsgrove House,
Ryelands Industrial Estate,
Bagley Road, Wellington, Somerset TA21 9PZ
Tel: 01823 653777 Fax: 01823 216796
email: sales@halsgrove.com

Part of the Halsgrove group of companies
Information on all Halsgrove titles is available at: www.halsgrove.com

Printed and bound in India by Replika Press Pvt. Ltd.

Introduction

As one of the earliest recorded towns in Britain, St Albans, known to the Romans as Verulamium, has had a long, colourful and distinguished history. It is certainly the oldest recorded town in Hertfordshire.

Dominated by the great Abbey Church of St Alban, this town has developed from a large thriving Roman town established in the first century AD in the valley of the Ver. The original Roman town was founded on the site of a Celtic settlement largely built of wood. This first town was destroyed by fire during the rebellion of Boudica in AD 60/61. After the defeat of the British queen, Verulamium was rebuilt in stone. By AD 275 the city was surrounded by walls and was able to boast a fine forum, a large basilica (city hall), temples, town houses and a theatre.

The Abbey itself, built on a hill to the east of the Roman town, was founded on the site of the first English martyrdom, that of Albanus, a Roman soldier who protected a priest of the Christian sect outlawed by the Romans. The monastery that grew up adjacent to the shrine was founded by Abbot Ulsinus in the early 900s. He was responsible for establishing a weekly market in the town which survives to this day. It was near St Albans that Nicholas Breakspear, the only English pope, grew up, although his application to join the Abbey was turned down. The power of the church was also demonstrated when St Albans became one of the five venues for the drafting of the Magna Carta in 1213.

As the town developed, tensions grew between the monastery and the townspeople. The Abbey was encircled by walls, of which the surviving Abbey Gateway is a reminder of the need to be protected from the town, which, in 1381, played a great part in The Peasants' Revolt. The Clock Tower, dating from the early 1400s, was a symbol of the townspeople's desire to show their independence from the Abbey. It wasn't until the Dissolution of the Monasteries that the differences between church and town were resolved.

St Albans took Parliament's side in the Civil War after the royalist High Sheriff was defeated by Oliver Cromwell and his men in a fight which took place near the Clock Tower.

In the eighteenth and early nineteenth centuries the town continued to grow. Brewing, straw hat making and brick making were among the industries which were followed here, and St Albans maintained its important position as a coaching town until the railway to London and to the North West was established in 1868. Further lines were later added, connecting the town to Watford and Hatfield. This expansion of transport and communications saw increased development to the east of the original settlement, and the town has been spreading ever eastwards ever since.

After much local interest and pressure the Abbey Church of St Alban became a cathedral in 1876, and St Albans became a city by royal charter.

These eventful centuries have left their mark on the architecture and environment of the town, from the remains of the Roman city of Verulamium and the later settlements of St Michael's to the mediaeval inns catering to pilgrims and the Georgian splendour of Fishpool Street.

Today the city of St Albans is still a thriving market town, a focus for commuters and a magnet for tourists. The arts and sciences are no strangers to the city. The film director, Stanley Kubrick, chose to live here, continuing a very long relationship between the city and the moving image. Arthur Melbourne-Cooper, one of the earliest film pioneers lived and worked here. Some examples of his work are screened in the City Museum. The children's author, Michael Morpurgo, was born here, and Stephen Hawking, the Cambridge theoretical physicist, grew up here, attending St Albans School.

In sporting circles the famous Ryder Cup golf tournament has its home here, at the Verulam Golf Course. The cup takes its name from the Ryder family.

The world of literature has not passed St Albans by. Charles Dickens located his 'Bleak House' here. He also described the brickmakers and their impoverished dwellings in his epic story of class, the legal profession and urban poverty, no doubt taking the brickworks on Bernards Heath as his inspiration.

In and around St Albans are such diverse features as the Cathedral, Roman Verulamium (walls, museum, hypocaust and theatre), the fifteenth-century clock tower, Waxhouse Gate, French Row, The Market Place, Verulam Park, Kingsbury Water Mill, St Albans Museum, The Organ Museum; and nearby, the Shenley Pastoral Centre, The De Havilland Aircraft Museum and Redbournbury Mill.

Our 'Portrait of St Albans' also extends to some of the villages and towns that surround the city: Wheathampstead, Park Street, London Colney, Colney Heath, Sandridge, Redbournbury and Harpenden. We have tried to capture a wide variety of images: parkland, open countryside, the public and private architecture from many periods, important interiors and historical artefacts, contemporary features and significant historical locations.

We are very grateful to the following for allowing us to take photographs: Lord and Lady Verulam (Roman Theatre), Justin Cross (St Albans Cathedral), Kate Warren and Mark Boyd (Verulamium and St Albans City Museums) and the management and staff of the following: St Albans Organ Museum, the De Havilland Heritage Museum, the Shenley Pastoral Centre, Future Gardens, the Gardens of the Rose, the Tourist Office and Redbournbury Mill.

We should also like to acknowledge the generous help and encouragement of our friends and family, and especially Chris and Betty Wedlake, David Massey, Jon Massey, Jennifer Carter, Rob and Dawn Stowe and Emily Stowe.

Choices, choices! One of the many colourful stalls on a market which can trace its origins back over a thousand years.

These brightly coloured rolls of fabric on a market stall remind us that St Albans is still a vibrant market town.

The old Town Hall by night. The building now hosts a restaurant, the Tourist Office and the restored courthouse.

French Row, possibly named from the French prisoners once kept there, is one of St Albans' best known side streets.

The Fleur-de-Lys inn in French Row has a long history. The original inn was built in the fifteenth century, but this incarnation dates from the sixteenth century. The king of France is said to have been held on this spot in 1356.

This busker has been a familiar figure on market days for many years.

Right: An unusual wooden carved figure at the rear of what was once the Christopher Inn.

Redbournbury Mill, the only working mill in the St Albans area.

Flour sacks at Redbournbury Mill.

The sack hoist machinery in motion at Redbournbury Mill.

Newly-baked loaves being removed from the oven on a baker's peel.

The Cathedral dominates the skyline, while many other periods of building development can be seen below it.

The eastern end of the Cathedral seen from Vintry Garden.

A single tree frames the St Albans skyline, as viewed from Watling Street.

The modern Christopher's Place shopping centre.

St Leonard's church in Sandridge basking in the morning sunshine.

The old tradition of the village pub next to the village church is well illustrated here in Sandridge.

Like many villages in Hertfordshire, Sandridge stretches itself out along the main road.

A chilly view across Verulam lakes.

A substantial section of the Roman wall of Verulamium, clearly showing its flint and tile layered construction.

The peace of Vintry Garden to the east of the Cathedral.

The majestic Clock Tower, built in the 1400s, is an imposing and familiar landmark for all who know the town.

Waxhouse Gate, which gets
its name from the candles sold
to pilgrims, leads down from the
High Street to the Cathedral.

The Clock Tower framed by Waxhouse Gate.

George Street by night, with the old Tudor Tavern bathed in the evening sun.

Originally the Abbey Gateway, this impressive building is now part of St Albans School.

Sumpter Yard, leading to the Cathedral from Holywell Hill was originally used to deliver supplies to the Abbey.

An architectural detail from
the north-eastern corner
of the Cathedral.

The southern aspect of the Cathedral showing some of the contrasting architectural styles, a distinct feature of this wonderful building.

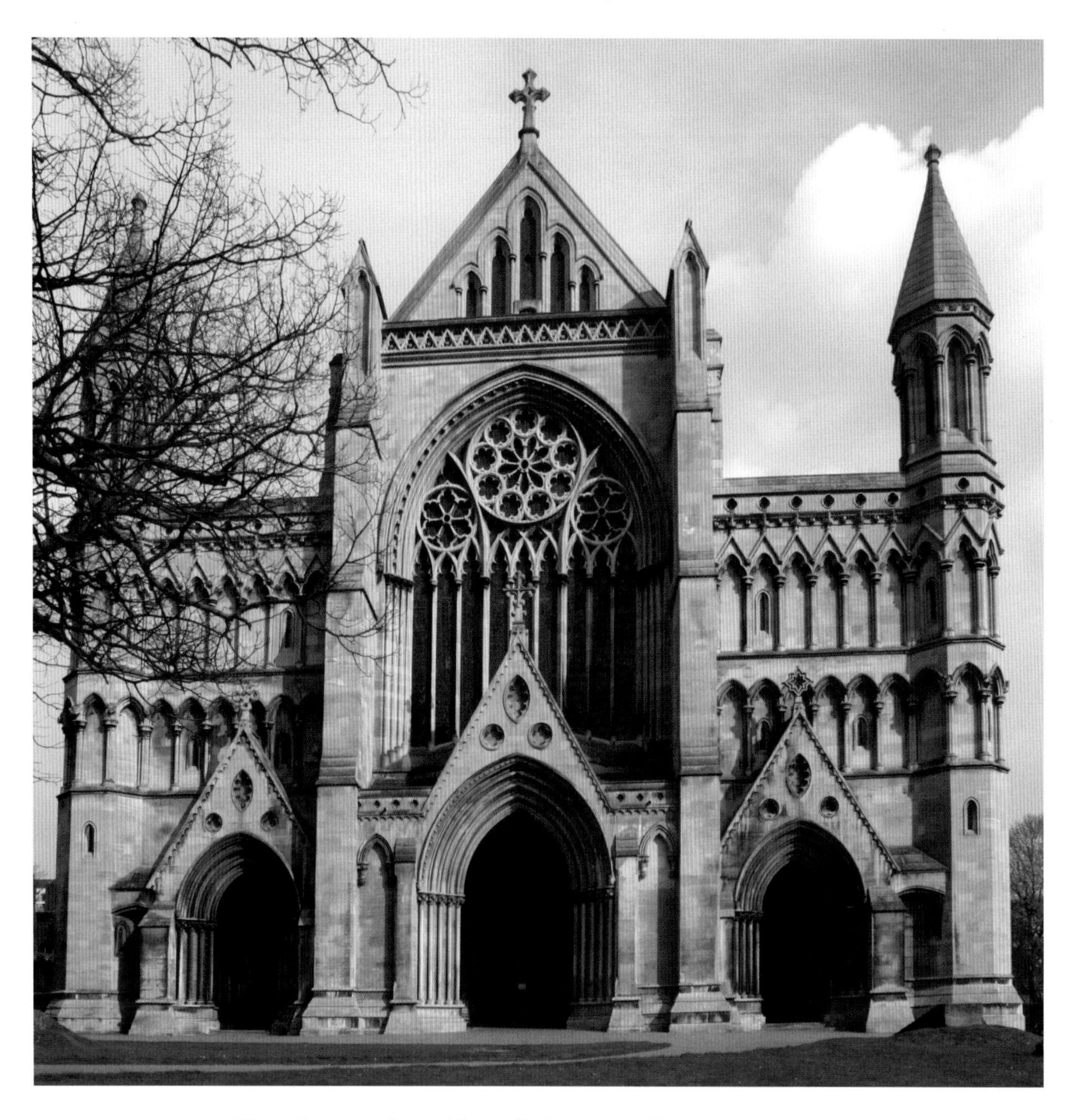

The striking west front of the Cathedral, restored by Grimthorpe in the nineteenth century, is one of the iconic images of the town.

The Norman tower of the Cathedral, built in part from the Roman brick and stonework salvaged from Verulamium.

New figures have replaced the images of saints on the nave screen destroyed in Henry VIII's Dissolution of the Monasteries. They represent (from the left): Ianani Luwum, Martin Luther King, Elizabeth of Russia, Alban, Amphibalus, Manche Masemola, Oscar Romero.

A fine view of the organ at the centre of the Cathedral.

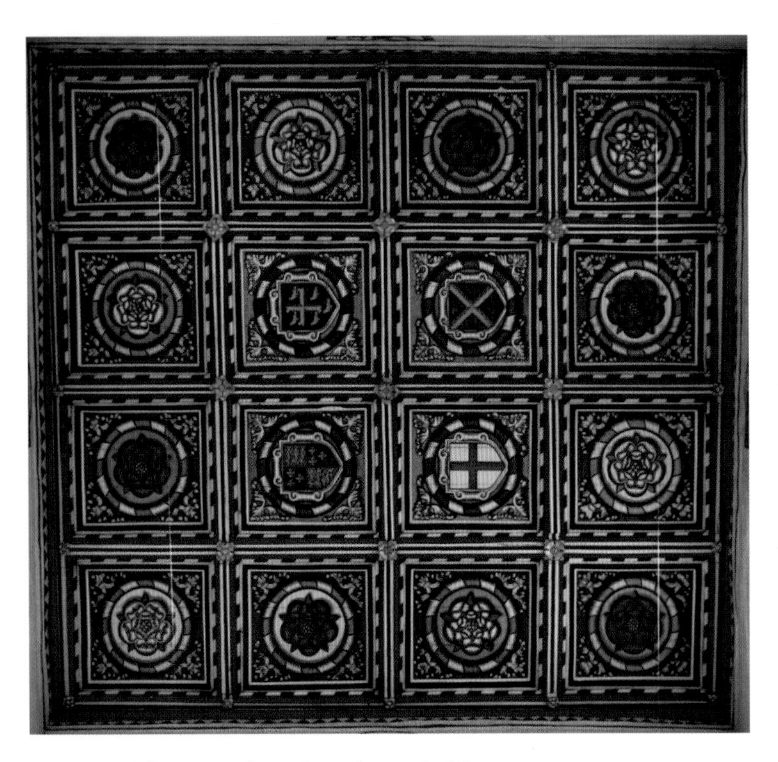

The painted panels in the roof of the tower are recent reconstructions. They include the gold cross on the blue background of St Alban himself, now the official arms of the city, and red and white roses, as a reminder of the city's involvement in the Wars of the Roses.

A section of a contemporary collage, made by children in the Education Centre, telling the story of the building of the new Abbey Church by Paul of Caen.

Stunning paintwork on the arches supporting the tower.

The vibrant colours of the recently restored
Rose Window in the north transept of the Cathedral.

Left: Modern refurbishment of the Cathedral has
uncovered some beautiful mediaeval paintings on the columns.

The magnificent high altar screen, dating originally from 1484 and much restored in the 1890s.

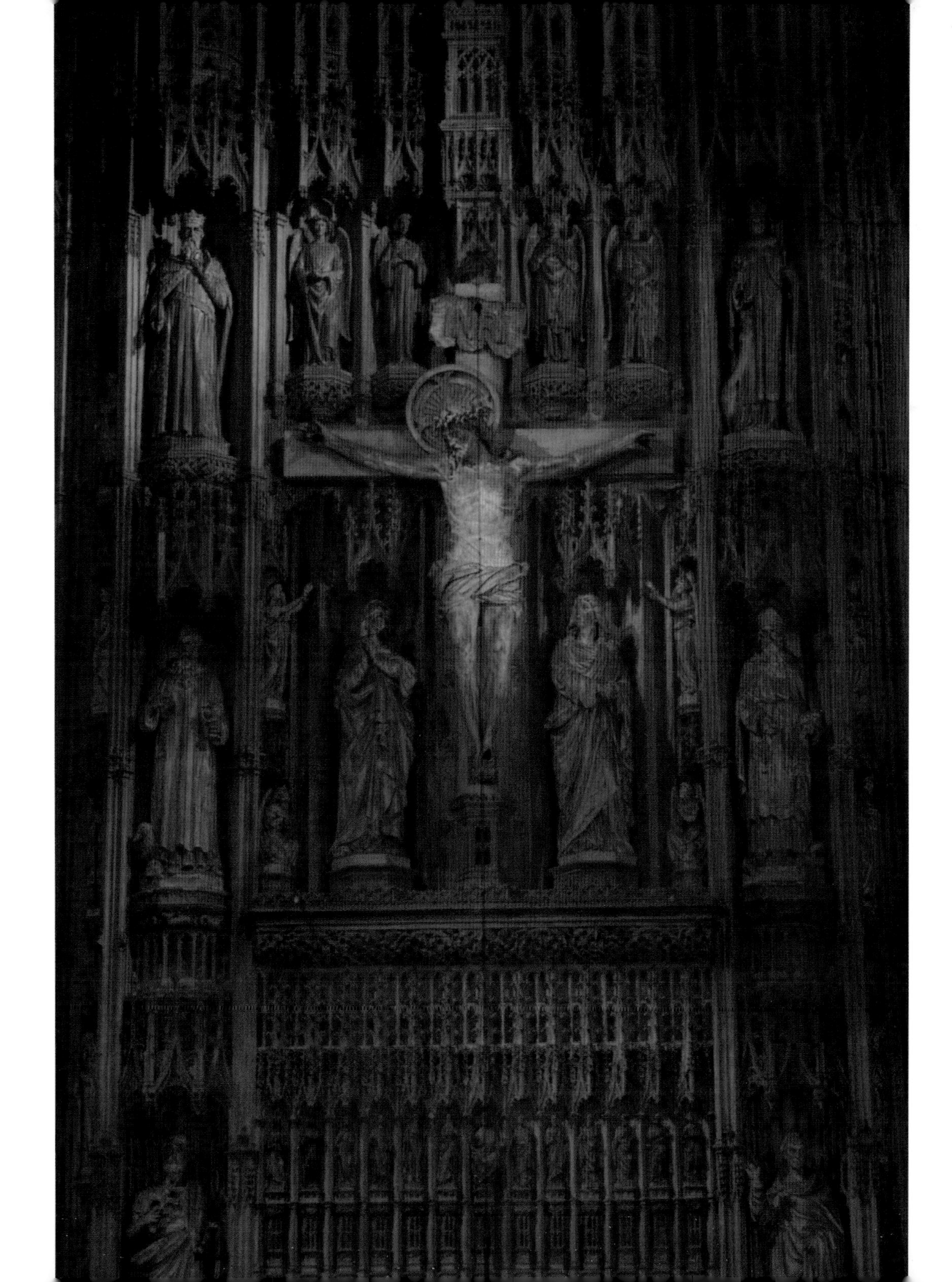

The shrine of St Alban, behind the high altar screen, venerated by pilgrims and worshippers for centuries, and restored in the last decade of the last century.

A striking statue of the Madonna and Child in the Lady Chapel.

The 'Cathedra' or bishop's throne, the all-important feature that makes the Abbey Church of St Alban a Cathedral, and St Albans a city.

Opposite:
A detail of the finely-carved marble tomb of Bishop Claughton.

A reconstruction of the fourteenth-century Wallingford Clock.

A close-up of the Wallingford Clock.

A quiet afternoon in Clarence Park, laid out in 1892.

A dramatic band's-eye view of the park from the Victorian bandstand.

Protecting the park, this house has a wonderful view of the gardens laid out within the park.

A welcome place for refreshment in a secluded corner off the High Street.

This building,
dating from the
seventeenth century
forms the
backdrop
to St Albans'
ancient market.

An original mediaeval window in one of two inns which were later joined together at the top of George Street. In the 1960s the building became the Tudor Tavern and is now a Thai restaurant.

Contrasting architectural styles grace Holywell Hill.

A secluded corner on busy Holywell Hill.

The White Hart on Holywell Hill, dating from the 1500s, was once an important coaching inn.

This striking building that now houses a restaurant was once Ryder's seed hall, and later a Royal Mail employees café.

The splendour of the Georgian and earlier timbered buildings of Fishpool Street, the oldest street name in St Albans, originally leading to the abbot's fishing pools at the bottom of the hill.

A beautiful stretch of the Ver descending from the Abbey Mill Stream.

The Fighting Cocks is said to be the oldest inhabited licensed premises in the country.

Another view of the lakes in Verulam Park, once the site of a Roman cemetery.

A view of the new from the old – the Cathedral, proudly standing on the brow of the hill, is glimpsed through the ruins of the Roman city wall.

A wealth of autumnal colours in Verulam Park dazzles the eye.

A dramatic view of the Cathedral tower by night.

Come face to face with a bewildering array of butterflies at the Butterfly World exhibit at Future Gardens.

A dramatic view of one of the Future Gardens at Chiswell Green.

This surreal sculpture, straight out of *The Borrowers*, is part of the Future Gardens exhibition in Chiswell Green.

This page and opposite:
The world-renowned Gardens of the Rose at Chiswell Green provides an ever-changing vista of colour and shape as different varieties of rose bloom at different times of the year.

One of the magnificent
blooms, Hot Chocolate,
which grace the
Gardens of the Rose at
Chiswell Green.

A magnificent arbour enticing the visitor to the Gardens of the Rose to explore the huge variety of blooms on display.

An attractive
timbered cottage
on Watling Street
at Park Street.

Oaklands Agricultural and Horticultural College has been housed here for many decades.

The striking entrance to
The Maltings Shopping Precinct.

Bold lines and dramatic windows provide
interesting reflections in The Maltings.

St Albans Golf Course, home of the Ryder Cup.

The Ver meanders through St Michaels.

Opposite: Shapes, light and reflections all come together to produce a stunning image of this modern office block just off the London Road.

The main entrance of the Shenley Pastoral Centre, near London Colney. It was originally built as an Anglican convent in the late nineteenth century.

Opposite:
St Michael's church, built in 948 on the site of the Roman basilica, or town hall, in the forum of Verulamium.

The very attractive chapel and grounds of the Pastoral Centre.

The glorious waterside greenery on the river at London Colney.

A view of the London Colney lakes, one of the town's lesser known attractions.

The parish church of St Peter at London Colney.

Models of wartime aircraft take wing in St Albans City Museum.

Salisbury Hall, near London Colney, is now best known for its connections to the aeronautical industry. It was here that the De Havilland Mosquito was designed.

AIR FRANCE
F-BGNX

The ruins of Sopwell House built in 1560 on the foundations of Sopwell Nunnery.

Opposite: The De Havilland Heritage Museum at Salisbury Hall houses
a fine collection of aircraft, including the first Mosquito.

The colourful hanging baskets decorate Redbourn High Street.

Cumberland House is a splendid Georgian town house fronting Redbourn High Street.

This Page And Opposite:
Redbourn Common or Heath dates back to pre-mediaeval times and was once thought to be the resting place of St Amphibalus, the Christian priest protected by Alban.

Cumberland Gardens in Redbourn provide a quiet retreat for visitors.

Albanians and visitors alike take refreshment in the Maltings Shopping Centre.

The very impressive entrance to Verulamium Museum, designed to represent a Roman building.

The magnificent 'shell' mosaic in Verulamium Museum.

Some splendid examples of Roman Samian Ware pottery in Verulamium Museum.

Below this splendid mosaic floor archaeologists discovered a hypocaust, the Roman underfloor central heating system.
In the far corners of this room can be seen the square flue pipes which took the hot air up the walls for extra comfort in our cold climate.

Top left: Coins featuring the head of the
Roman emperor, Antoninus Pius, in the Museum.

Above: The head of Neptune mosaic in Verulamium Museum.

Left: A detail of the intricate workmanship in this mosaic.

A view of the theatre from behind the stage area.

A general view of the Roman theatre, built around AD 150, showing the raised banks of the auditorium. This is the only example of a Roman theatre on display in Britain. It was used for animal fights and other such entertainments as well as dramatic performances.

The sixteenth century water mill at Kingsbury.

The front of the mill, with a large piece of Hertfordshire puddingstone on display.

Dramatic lighting emphasizes the machinery of the mill.

Three views of the splendid pageant held once a year to commemorate the martyrdom of St Alban at the hands of the Romans.

The old Corn Exchange, now a different kind of retail outlet.

The Hare and Hounds pub, dating from 1672, stands on the corner of Sopwell Lane, once the main London Road into St Albans.

The period car seems to match the timeless appeal of this side alley leading off George Street.

Part of the important Salaman Tool Collection on display in the City Museum.

A fine haul of
Mediaeval pottery
in the City Museum.

Left: A reconstructed
corner of Thrales
Tea Rooms, once
a thriving café in
St Peter's Street,
and familiar to
many local people.

A reminder that the old registry office was once a prison.

Other remains of the Roman city wall can be seen in Verulam Park.

May Cottage, a brick-and-timber construction, stands on Sopwell Lane.

Once the original railway terminus for St Albans, built in1858, this platform and shelter is now all that represents the Abbey Station.

Above: These colourful mosaics, created by the children of a local primary school, certainly cheer up what remains of the Abbey Station for early morning commuters to Watford and beyond.

Right: One of St Albans' 'out of the way' pubs, the White Hart Tap. This pub was originally connected to the White Hart in Holywell Hill by an extensive yard, now largely occupied by a car park.

Now converted, St Albans London Road Station was the first stop out of the town on the Hatfield branch line.

St Peter's church, at the top of St Peter's Street in the city, dates from the thirteenth century and provides a clerical counterpoint to the Cathedral.

The War Memorial stands at the head of St Peter's Street.

Bernards Heath, now a pleasant open space, was once a rubbish dump associated with the brick-making industry in the nineteenth century.

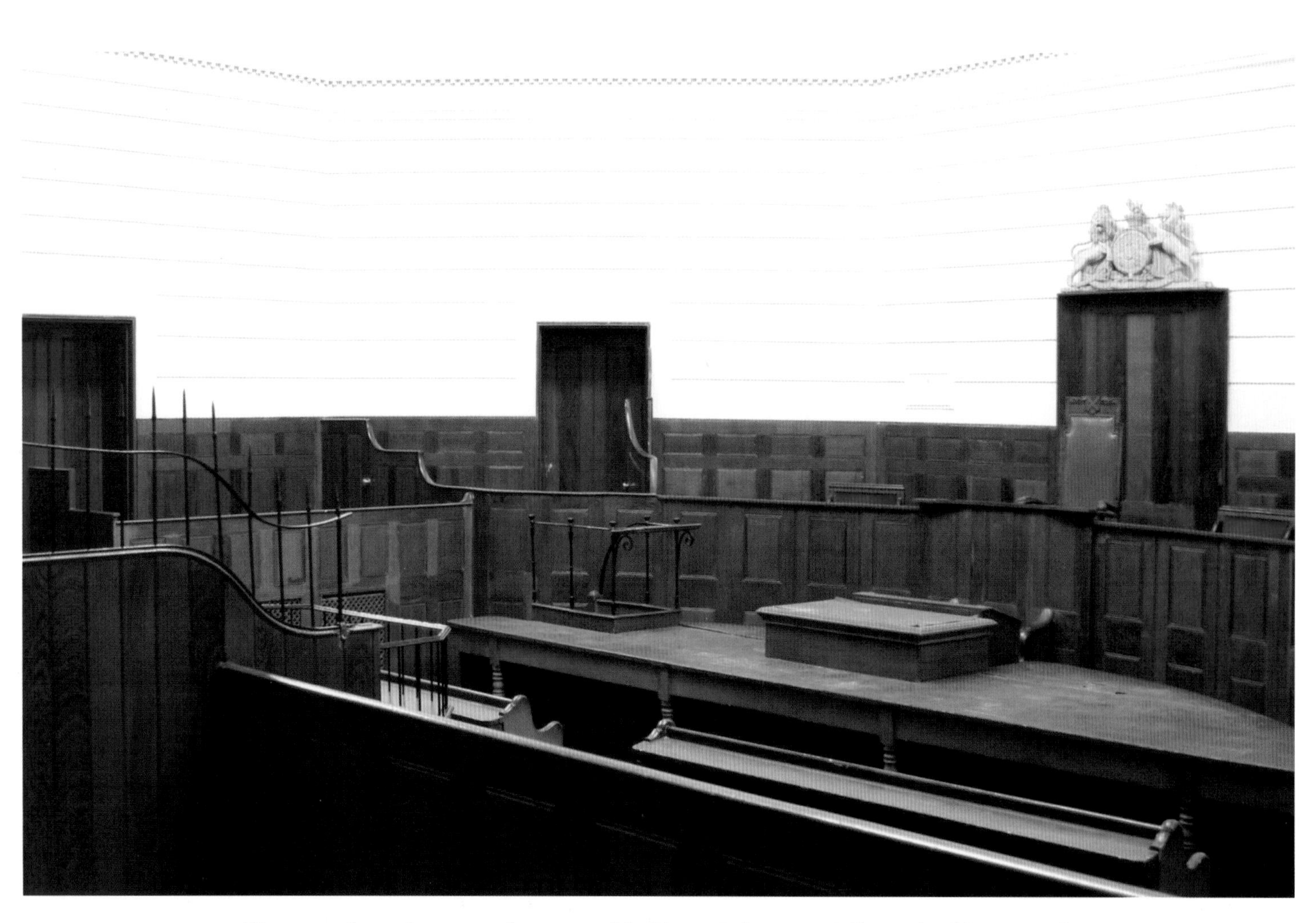

The restored court house now forms part of the Tourist Information Office in the old Town Hall.

Originally the Civic Hall, part of a central complex designed by Frederick Gibberd, the Arena is still a venue for performance events of all kinds.

Take a step back in time
along this little indoor avenue
of shops off the High Street.

The very attractive open space that is Hatching Green on the approach to Harpenden.

This page and opposite: The width of the old A6 running through Harpenden allows some very attractive garden developments in this old coaching town.

Rothamsted Research Institute is located in this idyllic setting in Harpenden.

Harpenden Common, an extensive stretch of public land, hosts a wide variety of wild life, and has been used in the past for horse-racing, fairs, ice-skating and hunting.

The River Lea passes tranquilly through Wheathampstead.

St Helen's parish church, Wheathampstead, dating from the thirteenth/fourteenth centuries.

The Bull, Wheathampstead, bathed in the evening sun. The inn dates back to the thirteenth century.

Opposite: A pastoral view over the open farmland near Wheathampstead.

Howzat? The classic image of the village cricket match, captured here at Wheathampstead.

Wide open spaces at Colney Heath.

A row of traditional houses in Lower Dagnall Street.

The colourful façade of a Belgian dancehall organ is a vivid feature of the St Albans Organ Museum in Camp Road.

Trains from Hatfield to St Albans would have steamed along this branch line and stopped at Smallford Station, whose platform is just visible beyond the bridge.

The local branch of Smiths occupies the old Moot Hall, and preserves features of an earlier era, such as the wooden-framed window-lights and the brightly painted sign.

The River Ver passes Kingsbury Mill at the bottom of Fishpool Street.

The dust rises as a tractor near Wheathampstead goes about its business of harvesting.

Many familiar landmarks in central St Albans can be seen from the Cathedral tower.

Romeland, seen from the green in front of the Cathedral.

This view of the south side of the Cathedral clearly shows the different styles of architecture which make up the complex structure of this imposing building.

The Cathedral by night.

The Cathedral is spotted through the autumnal leaves from a point where the Abbey itself once stood.

A night view of part of the buildings of St Albans School, one of the oldest in the country.

An almost magical sunset throws the Clock Tower and the Cathedral into stark silhouette.